BY SABRINA MESKO

HEALING MUDRAS
Yoga for Your Hands
Random House - Original edition

POWER MUDRAS
Yoga Hand Postures for Women
Random House - Original edition

MUDRA - GESTURES OF POWER
DVD - Sounds True

CHAKRA MUDRAS DVD set
HAND YOGA for Vitality, Creativity and Success
HAND YOGA for Concentration, Love and Longevity

HEALING MUDRAS
Yoga for Your Hands - New Edition

HEALING MUDRAS - 3 New Editions in full color:
Healing Mudras I. ~ For Your Body, II. ~ Mind, III. ~ Soul

POWER MUDRAS
Yoga Hand Postures for Women - New Edition

MUDRA THERAPY
Hand Yoga for Pain Management and Conquering Illness

YOGA MIND
45 Meditations for Inner Peace, Prosperity and Protection

MUDRAS FOR ASTROLOGICAL SIGNS
Volumes I. ~ XII.
MUDRAS for ARIES, TAURUS, GEMINI, CANCER, LEO, VIRGO,
LIBRA, SCORPIO, SAGITTARIUS, CAPRICORN, AQUARIUS, PISCES
12 Book Series

LOVE MUDRAS
Hand Yoga for Two

MUDRAS AND CRYSTALS
The Alchemy of Energy Protection

THE HOLISTIC CAREGIVER
A Guidebook for at-home care in late stage of Alzheimer's and dementia

MUDRAS

for

CANCER

By Sabrina Mesko Ph.D.H.

The material contained in this book has been written for informational purposes and is not intended as a substitute for medical advice nor is it intended to diagnose, treat, cure, or prevent disease. If you have a medical issue or illness, consult a qualified physician.

A Mudra Hands™ Book
Published by Mudra Hands Publishing
Arnica Press

Copyright © 2013, 2024 Sabrina Mesko Ph.D.H.

Photography by Mara
Animal photography by Sabrina Mesko
Illustrations by Kiar Mesko
Cover photo by Mara

Printed in the United States of America

ISBN-13:978-0615920894
ISBN-10:0615920896

For all my Cancer Friends

TABLE OF CONTENTS

THE MUDRA PRACTICE IS A
COMPLIMENTARY HEALING TECHNIQUE,
THAT OFFERS FAST AND EFFECTIVE
POSITIVE RESULTS.

MUDRAS WORK HARMONIOUSLY
WITH OTHER TRADITIONAL,
ALTERNATIVE AND COMPLEMENTARY
HEALING PROTOCOLS.

THEY HELP RESTORE DEPLETED
SUBTLE ENERGY STATES
AND OPTIMIZE THE PRACTITIONER'S
OVERALL STATE OF WELLNESS.

Mudras for CANCER

JUNE 22 - JULY 22

BODY
Chest, breasts

PLANET
Moon

COLORS
Silver, gray

ELEMENT
Water

STONES and GEMS
Pearl

ANIMAL
Creatures with shell

Introduction

Ever since I can remember, I have been fascinated by the never-ending view of the stars in the sky and the presence of other mysterious planets. As a child I wondered for hours about where does the Universe end and when my Father explained the possibility that time and space exist in a very different way than we imagined, my mind went wild with possibilities. I was however quite skeptical about astrology in general until one day in my early youth, a dear friend introduced me to a true Master of Vedic Astrology. He quickly and completely diminished any of my doubts about how precise certain facts can be revealed in one's Celestial map.

It was as if an invisible veil had been removed, and I was granted a peek over to the other side. The astrologer also adamantly pointed out that nothing is written in stone and one's destiny has a lot of space to navigate thru. You can make the best of the situation if you know your given parameters. My fascination and use of astrological science continues to this day and compliments and enriches my work with other observation techniques that I use when consulting.

One is born with character aspects and potential for realization of mapped-out future events, but there is always a possibility that another road may be taken. This has to do with the choices we make. Free will is given to all of us, even though often the choices we have seem to be very limited. But still, the choices are always there, forcing us to consciously participate and eventually take responsibility for our decisions, actions, and consequences.

The science of Astrology has been around for millenniums and even though some people are still doubtful, I always remind them that there is no disputing the fact, that the Moon affects the high and low tide of our Oceans - hence our bodies consisting mostly of water are affected by planetary movements in many fascinating and profound ways. Even the biggest skeptic agrees with that fact.

The Love of the Universal Power for each one of us is unconditional, everlasting and omnipresent. No matter what kind of life-journey you have, it is the very best one designed especially for you, rest assured. And when you are experiencing life's various challenges and wishing for a smooth ride instead, keep in mind that a life filled with lessons is a life fulfilling its purpose. The tests you encounter in your daily life are your opportunities. The wisdom learned is your asset, and the experiences gained are your wealth. Your Spirit's abundance is measured by the battles you fought and how you fought them. Did you help others and leave this world a better place in any way? Your true intention matters more than you know.

Each one of us has a very unique-one of a kind celestial map placed gently, but firmly and irrevocably into effect at the precise time of our birth. There are certain aspects of one's chart that reveal possible character tendencies and predisposed behavior regarding love, partnerships, maintaining one's health, pursuit of success and a way of communicating. The benefits of knowing and understanding the effects of your chart on various aspects of your life can be profound. It can help you understand and prepare ahead of time for certain circumstances that are coming your way, which increases the possibility of a better quality of life in general.

If you knew that a specific time period could be beneficial for your career, wouldn't it be good to know that ahead of your plans? If you are aware that certain aspects of your physical constitution are predisposed to a weakness or sensitivity, wouldn't it be beneficial to pay attention and prevent a possible future health ailment?

If you can foresee that a certain time will be slower for you in achieving positive results, wouldn't it be wise to use that time for preparation for a more fortuitous timing? How many times have you attempted to pursue a dream of yours that just didn't seem to want to happen? And when you were completely exhausted and disillusioned, the fortunate opportunity presented itself, except now you were tired, overwhelmed and had no energy or enthusiasm left. Having such information ahead of time would offer you the chance to save your energy during quiet, less active time, so that when your luck is more likely, you can seize the opportunity and make the most of it.

Mudras will forever fascinate me, and I have been humbled and excited how many practitioners from around the world have written to me, grateful to have these techniques and most importantly really experiencing positive effects in time of need. Therefore, it has been a natural idea for me to combine these two of my favorite topics and create a series of Mudra sets for all twelve Astrological signs.

The Mudras depicted in this book are specifically selected for the astrological sign of Aries, with intention to help you maximize your gifts and soften the challenges that your celestial map contains.

It is important to know that each astrological chart – celestial map – contains information that can be used beneficially and there are no "bad signs" or "better sings". Your chart is unique as are you. By gaining information, knowledge and understanding what the placements of the planets offer you, your path to self-knowledge is strengthened.

I hope this book will attract astrology readers as well as meditation and yoga practitioners and help you utilize the beneficial combination of both these fascinating techniques. Knowledge will help you experience the very best possible version of your life. The biggest mystery in your life is You. Discover who you are and enjoy the journey.

And remember, no matter what life presents you with, don't forget to smile and keep a happy heart. With each experience gained you are spiritually wealthier for it. And that my friend, stays with you forever. The wisdom gained is eternally imprinted in your soul.

Blessings,

Sabrina

MUDRAS

Mudras are movements involving only fingers, hands and arms. Mudras originated in ancient Egypt where they were practiced by high priests and priestesses in sacred rituals. Mudras can be found in every culture of the world. We all use Mudras in our everyday life when gesturing while communicating and when holding our hands in various intuitive positions. Mudras used in yoga practice offer great benefits and have a tremendously positive effect on our overall state of well-being. By connecting specific fingertips and your palms in various Mudra positions, you are directly affecting complex energy currents of your subtle energy body. As numerous energy currents run thru your brain centers, Mudras help stimulate specific areas for an overall state of emotional, physical and mental well-being.

INSTRUCTIONS FOR MUDRA PRACTICE

YOUR BODY POSTURE
During the Mudra practice sit in an upright position with a straight spine, with both your feet on the ground or in a cross-legged position. Comfort is essential so that you may practice undisturbed and focus on proper practice positions.

YOUR EYES
Keep your eyes closed and gently lightly lift the gaze above the horizon.

WHERE
For achieving best results of ideal Mudra practice, it is essential that you find a peaceful place, without distractions.

Once your Mudra practice is established, you can practice Mudras anywhere.

WHEN
You may practice Mudras at any time. Best times for practice are first thing in the morning and at bedtime. Avoid practicing Mudras on a full stomach, and after a big meal wait for an hour before practice.

HOW LONG
Each Mudra should be practiced for at least 3 minutes at a time. Ideal practice is 3 Mudras for 3 minutes each with a follow-up short 3 minutes of complete stillness, peace and meditation or reflection.

HOW OFTEN
You may practice Mudras every day. Explore various Mudras by selecting a Mudra that fits your specific needs for any given day.

BREATH CONTROL

Proper breathing is essential for optimal Mudra practice. There are two main breathing techniques that can be used with your practice.

LONG DEEP SLOW BREATH
Slowly and deeply inhale thru your nose while relaxing and expanding the area or your solar plexus and lower stomach. Exhale thru the nose slowly, while gently contracting the stomach area and pulling your stomach in. Pace your breathing slowly and notice the immediate calming effects. This breathing technique is appropriate for relaxation, inducing calmness and peace.

BREATH OF FIRE

Inhale and exhale thru the nose at a much faster pace while practicing the same concept of expanding navel area and contracting with each exhalation. Unless otherwise noted Mudras are generally practiced with the long, deep slow breath. The breath of fire has an energizing, recharging effect on body and is to be used only when so noted.

CHAKRAS

Along our spine, starting at the base and continuing up towards the top of your head, lie subtle energy centers – vortexes – called charkas, that have a powerful effect on the overall state of your health and well-being. The practice of Mudras profoundly affects the proper function of these energy centers and magnifies their power.

Our subtle energy body is highly sensitive to outside sensory stimuli of sound, aromas, visuals and outside electric currents that constantly surround us. Frequencies that permeate specific locations may attract or bother you. Perhaps you may feel eager to stay somewhere where the energy suits you and yet feel suffocated when the environment does not agree with you. We are all sensitive to energies, but some of us feel them more than others.

A positive blend of energies with another person can create a magnet-like effect, whereas another person's negative unharmonious subtle energy field subconsciously pushes you away.

By leading healthy lives and optimizing the proper function of charkas, you empower your subtle energy bodies adding strength to your physical body, mind and spirit. Destructive behavior like addictions and abuse weaken your Auric field and "leak" your vital energy. By maintaining a healthy Aura-energy field, you can fine-tune your natural capacity for "sensing" places, situations and people that compliment your energy frequency. In a state of "clean energy" you achieve capacity for high awareness and become your own best guide.

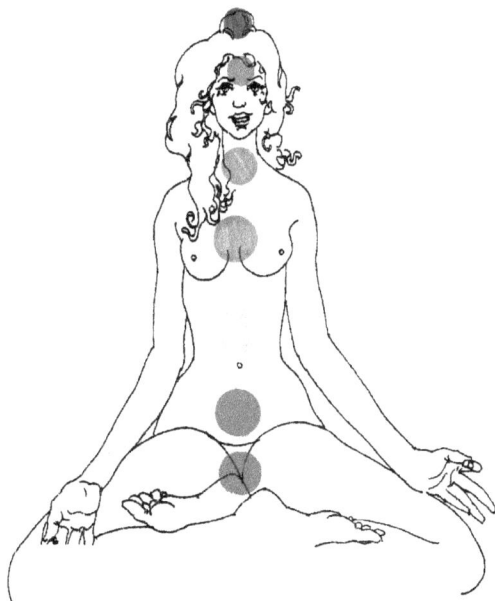

CHAKRAS IN THE BODY

Base Chakra: Foundation
Second Chakra: Sexuality
Third Chakra: Ego
Fourth Chakra: Love
Fifth Chakra: Truth
Sixth Chakra: Intuition
Seventh Chakra: Divine Wisdom

FIRST CHAKRA
LOCATION: Base of the spine
GLAND: Gonad
COLOR: Red
REPRESENTS:
Foundation, shelter, survival,
courage, inner security, vitality

SECOND CHAKRA
LOCATION: Sex organs
GLAND: Adrenal
COLOR: Orange
REPRESENTS:
Creative expression, sexuality,
procreation, family

THIRD CHAKRA
LOCATION: Solar plexus
GLAND: Pancreas
COLOR: Yellow
REPRESENTS:
Ego, intellect, emotions of fear and anger

FOURTH CHAKRA
LOCATION: Heart
GLAND: Thymus
COLOR: Green
REPRESENTS:
All matters of the heart, love,
self-love, compassion and faith

FIFTH CHAKRA
LOCATION: Throat
GLAND: Thyroid
COLOR: Blue
REPRESENTS:
Communication, truth,
higher knowledge, your voice

SIXTH CHAKRA
LOCATION: Third Eye
GLAND: Pineal
COLOR: Indigo
REPRESENTS:
Intuition, inner vision, the Third eye

SEVENTH CHAKRA
LOCATION: Top of the head - Crown
GLAND: Pituitary
COLOR: White and Violet
REPRESENTS:
The universal God consciousness,
the heavens, unity

NADIS

Your subtle energy body contains an amazing network of electric currents called Nadis. There are 72.000 energy currents that run throughout your body from toes to the top of your head as well as your fingertips. These channels of light must be clear and vibrant with life force for your optimal health and empowerment. With regular Mudra practice you can open, clear, reactivate and re-energize your energy currents.

Your Hands and Fingers

While practicing Mudras you are magnifying the effects of the Solar system on your physical, mental and spiritual body. Each finger is influenced by the following planets:

THE THUMB - MARS

THE INDEX FINGER – JUPITER

THE MIDDLE FINGER – SATURN

THE RING FINGER – THE SUN

THE LITTLE FINGER – MERCURY

MANTRA

Combining the Mudra practice with appropriate Mantras magnifies the beneficial effects of these ancient self-healing techniques.

The hard palate in your mouth has 58 energy meridian points that connect to and affect your entire body.

By singing, speaking or whispering Mantras, you touch these energy points in a specific order that is beneficial and has a harmonious and healing effect on your physical, mental and spiritual state.

The ancient science of Mantras helps you reactivate nadis, magnifies and empowers your energy field, improves your concentration and stills your mind.

About Astrology

The word Horoscope originates from a Latin word ORA – hour and SCOPOS – view. One could presume that Horoscope means "a look into your hour of birth." The precise moment of your birth determines your celestial set-up. An accurate astrological chart can reveal most detailed aspects of your life, your character, your gifts, your future possible events, challenges that await you, lucky events that are bestowed upon you, and your outlook for happy relationships, successful careers, accomplishments, health and many possible variations of life events. I say possible, because your decisions will determine the outcome.

There are 12 signs in the Zodiac and your birthday reflects the position of your Sun sign. The specific positions of other planets in your chart are calculated considering the precise moment – hour and minute and of course location of your birth. The birth time will reveal your Rising or Ascending sign, which will further determine other essential facts of your chart.

The constant transitional movements of the Planets affect each one of us differently, a time that may be difficult for some may prove supremely lucky for another and yet we are all interconnected by mutual effects of continuous planetary movements. Nothing is standing still; the changes are ongoing. On a different note, a few slow-moving planets connect us in other ways, as they keep certain generations under specific aspects and influences. We are all inseparable and in continuous motion.

There are numerous fascinating ways to use astrology and there is no doubt that the constant motion of all these powerful and majestic Planets in our Solar system affect each and every one of us differently. Astrology can be used as an additional tool to help you continue progressing on the mysterious life journey of self-discovery and self-realization.

Remember, the power of decision is yours as is the responsibility for consequences. Make peace with your doubts, pursue your dreams and relish in results.

When the outcome is less than what you expected, learn to pick yourself up and continue on, wiser with knowledge you gained, that alone being a good reason for remaining optimistic. When the outcome surpasses your expectations, well, then you will know what to do…mostly take a breath, smile, and enjoy the moment.

YOUR SUN SIGN

There are 12 signs in the Zodiac. The day of your birth determines your Sun-sign. Most often this is the extent of average person's knowledge and interest in astrology. However, the other aspects in the astrological chart are equally as important and need to be taken into consideration.

In this book your main guide is your Sun sign's dispositions, tendencies, weaknesses and gifts. Certainly, there are endless combinations of charts, and your Sun sign alone will not reveal the complete picture of your celestial map. For more detailed information and reflection about your chart, you need to know your ascending-rising sign.

YOUR ASCENDING-RISING SIGN

Your rising sign, also known as the ascendant, reflects the degree of ecliptic rising over the eastern horizon at the precise moment of your birth. It reveals the foundation of your personality. That means that even if you have the same birthday with someone else, your time of birth would create completely different aspects and influences in your chart. No two people are alike. You are one of a kind and so is everyone else. However, you may have some strong similarities and timing aspects that will be often alike. Your rising sign also reveals the basis of your chart and House placements. Your rising sign determines and is in your first house. There are 12 Houses and each depicts precise in-depth information about all aspects of your physical life, emotional make and character tendencies. It is incredibly complex and fascinating. Regarding your Mudra practice in combination with your Astrological Sign, it would be beneficial to know also your Rising sign and apply Mudras that empower your Rising sign as well. For example, if your Sun sign is CANCER, but your rising sign is Libra, it would be most beneficial to practice Mudra sets for both signs.

HOW TO USE THIS BOOK

In each book of the *Mudras for the Astrological Signs* series, you will find Mudras for different astrological signs that will help you in most important areas of your life: Health, Love, Success, and Overcoming your challenging qualities. We all have them, as we also all have gifts. This book is specific for the sign of Aries. You may change your Mudra practice daily as needed, and keep in mind, that certain habits or tendencies need a longer time to adjust, change, and improve. Be patient, kind, and loving towards yourself.

MUDRAS

for TRANSCENDING

CHALLENGES

Each one of us has a few character tendencies or weaknesses that are connected to our astrological chart. To help you transcend, overcome and redirect these challenges into your beneficial assets, you can use the Mudras in this chapter.

MUDRA FOR
INNER SECURITY

You are emotionally very sensitive and loving. That is an endearing quality and gives you the capacity for compassion for all living creatures and special sense of protection for your close family. But that aspect can cause you to emotionally swing the other way and be over touchy and perhaps even moody. You need to empower your emotional inner security and stability and this Mudra will help you achieve just that.

CHAKRA: 3, 4

COLOR: Yellow, green

MANTRA:

AD SHAKTI AD SHAKTI

(I Bow to the Creator's Power)

Sit with a straight back, place your hands in reversed prayer pose, hands touching back-to-back at the level of your heart and solar plexus. Hold the pose for one and a half minutes, then repeat with the palms pressed together in a prayer pose.

BREATH: Long, deep and slow.

MUDRA FOR
SELF-CONFIDENCE

When emotions run deep your entire physical body and your mind are affected. This may cause you feeling less secure and confident thus propelling your cautious nature even deeper into that direction. Your strong and vivid imagination plays a role as well and it is very important to balance your self-confidence and stability as a part of your daily routine. This Mudra will help you establish a firm and confident disposition which will work wonderfully with your other lovely qualities.

CHAKRA : 3, 6

COLOR: Yellow, indigo

MANTRA:

**EK ONG KAR SAT GURU PRASAD
SAT GURU PRASAD EK ONG KAR**
(The Creator Is the One That Dispels Darkness
and Illuminates Us by His Grace)

Sit with a straight back. Lift your hands up to the level of your solar plexus with elbows bent to the sides. Bend the middle, ring, and little fingers and touch them back-to-back. Extend the index fingers and thumbs and press them together. The thumbs are pointed toward you and the index fingers away from you.

BREATH: Long, deep and slow.

MUDRA FOR
DIMINISHING WORRIES

Your great love and deep caring nature for your family brings along also some worry and unrest. Very often you will find yourself in a situation to be taking care of your entire extended family and overseeing and guiding everyone thru their life journeys. Naturally an element of clinginess could be present, and it is important to learn to let the birds fly out of the nest as well. They will always return to you for advice, that will never change. But endless worrying won't do, therefore this Mudra will help you overcome that tendency, so that you too can breathe, and enjoy life.

CHAKRA: 4, 5, 6

COLOR: Green, blue, indigo

Sit with a straight back. Bring your hands in front of your chest with the palms facing up. The sides of the little fingers and inner sides of the palms are touching. Now bring the middle fingertips together, perpendicular to the palms. Extend the thumbs away from the palm. Hold and keep the fingers stretched as little antennas for energy.

BREATH: Long, deep and slow.

MUDRAS
for HEALTH
and BEAUTY

Each astrological sign rules certain areas of your body. The Mudras in this chapter will help you strengthen your physical weaknesses while maintaining a healthy body, and a beautiful, vibrant appearance.

MUDRA FOR
EMOTIONAL BALANCE

Your gifts and intuitive powers require a clear calm instrument in order to operate at maximum capacity. Emotions need to be in perfect balance for you to be able to tune-in and sense proper decisions, future events and opportunities. In the area of your health, it is essential that you protect yourself from unnecessary emotional stress and everything that it brings along. This Mudra will work wonders for your overall emotional state and comfort. With regular practice you will be able to magnify your intuition while preserving your health.

CHAKRA : All

COLOR: All

MANTRA:

SAT NAM
(Truth is God's Name, One in Spirit)

Before you practice this Mudra, drink a glass of room temperature water to balance your system. Sit with a straight spine. Place both hands with palms open under your armpits. Close your eyes, inhale and give yourself a big hug and lift the shoulders toward the ears for a few moments and then lower your shoulders, exhale, relax and open your eyes. Repeat at an easy pace for three minutes.

BREATH: Long, deep and slow.

MUDRA FOR
STRONG NERVES

Your rich emotions and sympathetic nature will often get you into situations of fighting for others, weaker than yourself while protecting them from harm. This requires a certain level of energy and perseverance that wears on your nervous system. In order to maintain a healthy physical state in that area, you need to pay special attention to protecting and preserving your nervous system. This Mudra offers you great help with this aspect and requires regular practice, in completely peaceful environment, and with focused attention. Do not forget to be as concerned about your welfare as you are for that of others. You can only help them if you remain strong and healthy yourself - in body, mind and spirit.

CHAKRA : 3, 4

COLOR: Yellow, green

Sit with a straight spine. Lift your left hand at ear level, palm facing out. Connect the thumb and middle finger and stretch out other fingers. Place your right hand in front of the solar plexus, palm facing up. The thumb and little finger are touching while other fingers are straight. **This position is reversed for men.**

BREATH: Long, deep and slow.

MUDRA FOR
REMOVING DEPRESSION

By knowing you are vulnerable and prone to emotional mood swings, you can prepare and prevent this occurrence from happening. Proper diet is essential as is sufficient rest and relaxation. If you ignore these vulnerable aspects, you could unnecessarily suffer from depression, which would require more work and discipline to overcome. Therefore, it is most beneficial, that you establish heathy habits and proper care for yourself in every aspect-with a healthy lifestyle and environment.

CHAKRA : 4, 5, 6

COLOR: Green, blue, indigo

MANTRA:

HARI NAM SAT NAM
SAT NAM HARI NAM
(God is Truth in Creation)

Sit with a straight spine. Stretch your arms in front of you, hands up at heart level. Put the backs of your hands together, with your fingers pointing away from your body, making sure that as many as possible knuckles touch. Your forearms are as parallel to the ground as possible, thumbs pointing down to the ground. This Mudra creates a great deal of tension on the back part of your hands, but do not practice too long if your muscles are straining.

BREATH: Long, deep and slow.

MUDRAS
for LOVE

The Mudras in this chapter will help you understand your love temperament, your expectations, your longings and how to attract the optimal love partner into your life. It is most beneficial to know how others perceive you in the matters of the heart. It will also help you understand your partner and their astrologically influenced love map.

MUDRA FOR RELEASING GUILT

You are a wonderful and caring partner, reliable and filled with pure love. You create ever new romantic situations and are eager to care for children and family. Sometimes you may become overly sentimental about the past and struggle to move on as life inevitably does. The old days were romantic, but so can be today. With this strong tendency to hang on to the past, you may carry along some unnecessary feelings of guild and take on your shoulders more responsibility than appropriate. This Mudra will help you prevent that from happening and help you enjoy your love life without unnecessary self-inflicted burdens.

CHAKRA : 3

COLOR: Yellow

MANTRA:

I AM THINE WAHE GURU
(I am Thine, Divine Teacher within)

Sit with a straight back, elbows out to the sides, and bring your palms up to the level between your stomach and heart center. Palms are facing up toward the sky, right hand resting in left. Upper arms are slightly away from the body. Breathe slowly and deeply.

BREATH: Long, deep and slow.

MUDRA FOR HAPPINESS

Being in the here and now and enjoying every second of it-
that is the key. After you have taken care of everything and
everybody, be present with your lover and enjoy the supremely
blissful romantic environment you helped create. This is what
love is all about. Toss the worry, nothing else matters. This
Mudra will help you learn how to enjoy these moments of
profound happiness that will forever imprint in your spirit,
mind and heart, and carry you thru thick and thin. That's what
pure love is-everlasting and forever.

CHAKRA : 4

COLOR: Green

MANTRA:
SAT NAM
(Truth is God's Name, One in Spirit)

Sit with a straight spine. Bend your elbows and bring your arms to your sides, away from your body. Elbows are just below the level of the shoulders. Palms are facing forward. Stretch the index and middle fingers and bend the ring and little fingers, pressing them into the palms firmly with the thumbs. Hold for three minutes and relax.

BREATH: Long, deep and slow.

MUDRA FOR
PREVENTING STRESS

Often stress is something we create out of unnecessary habits or situations. When various challenging dynamics present themselves to you, you have a choice. What is truly important and worth your time and effort? You cannot protect every single vulnerable human being or living creature, so be selective to make an impact and reserve the rest of your energy for yourself and your loved ones. You are a delicate instrument and for optimal health stress needs to be eliminated as much as possible. Make time for loving home environment that will heal and empower you.

CHAKRA : 3

COLOR: Yellow

Sit with a straight spine. Bend your elbows and bring your forearms in front of your solar plexus area parallel to the ground. Rest the back of the left hand in the palm of the right hand, both palms facing up. Fingers are straight and together. Hold for three minutes and concentrate on your breath.

BREATH: Long, deep and slow.

MUDRAS
for SUCCESS

The Mudras in this chapter will offer you tools to present yourself to the world in your optimal light. Often one is confused in which direction to turn or where their strength lies. Mudras will help you focus and remember your essential creative desires; help you gain self-confidence and inner security to recognize your desired and destined path. If you know what you want, and your purpose is harmonious for the better good of all, your success is within reach.

MUDRA
FOR PROSPERITY

You have an excellent sense for business and can be extremely shrewd. The financial matters are important to you, and you take security very seriously. Thru it all, fulfillment is more important to you than pure ambition and when you find your joy in your work, you like stability and continuity. This Mudra will help you establish and attract a prosperous mental disposition and environment to secure the stable life that you need and desire.

CHAKRA : 1, 2, 3,

COLOR: Red, orange, yellow

MANTRA:

HAR HAR
(God, God)

Sit with a straight back. Bring your hands in front of you, fingers together and palms facing down. Press the sides of the index fingers together and hold for a second. Now flip your hands over o that the palms are facing up toward the sky for a second and the edges of the little fingers are touching. Keep repeating and chant the mantra HAR with each change of hand position. Continue the practice for eleven minutes and rest.

BREATH: Short, fast breath of fire from the point of the navel, repeated with each mantra and Mudra movement.

MUDRA FOR A CALM MIND

When you are closing that major business deal and can taste the sweet flavor of success, it is most important that the emotions do not get the best of you and suddenly expose you as a vulnerable, overly sensitive creature that you are. Keeping a calm mind becomes a priority and with that accomplished you can master any situation anytime, anyplace. This Mudra will help you maintain a serene and peaceful state of mind and can be practiced even during a business meeting.

CHAKRA : 3, 4, 6

COLOR: Yellow, green, Indigo

MANTRA:
OM
(God in His Absolute State)

Sit with a straight spine. Cross your arms in front of your chest, elbows bent at a ninety-degree angle and arms parallel to the ground. The right hand is on top of the left arm and left hand below the right arm. All fingers are together and straight. Hold and keep the arms from sinking for three minutes then relax and be still.

BREATH: Long, deep and slow.

MUDRA FOR
MENTAL BALANCE

We all know that emotional and mental states are closely interconnected-in your case even more so. That presents a possible situation of your emotions taking over even when it may be to your disadvantage. Be in charge and a master of your emotions-this way your mind will be able to work to its fullest and greatest potential. Let your mental brilliance have an opportunity to shine. To assure that you are prepared and take advantage for every professional golden opportunity, practice this Mudra and maintain optimal mental clarity and unwavering balance. Success is assured.

CHAKRA : All

COLOR: All

MANTRA:
**GOBINDAY, MUKUNDAY, UDAARAY, APAARAY,
HARYNG,KARYNG,NIRNAMAY, AKAMAY**
(Sustainer, Liberator, Enlightener, Infinite,
Destroyer, Creator, Nameless, Desireless)

Sit with a straight spine. Place your hands at solar plexus level in front of you and interlace the fingers backward with palms facing up. Fingers are pointing up and the thumbs are straight.

BREATH: Long, deep and slow.

ABOUT THE AUTHOR

SABRINA MESKO Ph.D.H. is an International and Los Angeles Times bestselling author of the timeless classic *Healing Mudras - Yoga for your Hands* translated into fourteen languages. She authored over twenty books on Mudras, Mudra Therapy, Mudras and Astrology, Holistic Caregiving, Spirituality and Meditation techniques.

Sabrina holds a Bachelors Degree in Sensory Approaches to Healing, a Masters in Holistic Science, a Doctorate in Ancient and Modern Approaches to Healing, and a Ph.D.H in Healtheoloyy from the American Institute of Holistic Theology. She is board certified from the American Alternative medical Association and American Holistic Health Association.

She has been featured in media outlets such as The Los Angeles Times, CNBC News, Cosmopolitan, the cover of London Times Lifestyle, The Discovery Channel documentary on Hands, W magazine, First for Women, Health, Web-MD, Daily News, Focus, Yoga Journal, Australian Women's weekly, Blend, Daily Breeze, New Age, the Roseanne Show and various international live television programs. Her articles have been published in world-wide publications.

She hosted her own weekly TV show educating about health, well-being and complementary medicine. She is an executive member of the World Yoga Council and has led numerous international Yoga Therapy educational programs. She directed and produced her interactive double DVD titled *Chakra Mudras* - a Visionary awards finalist.

Sabrina also created award winning international Spa and Wellness Centers and is a motivational keynote conference speaker addressing large audiences all over the world.

She is the founder of Arnica Press, a boutique Book Publishing House. Her mission is to discover, mentor, nurture and publish unique authors with a meaningful message, that may otherwise not have an opportunity to be heard. She is the founder of world's only online Mudra Teacher and Mudra Therapy Education, Certification and Mentorship program, with her certified therapists spreading these ancient teachings in over 28 countries around the world.

www.SabrinaMesko.com